Why Hypnotism Works!

Frank Q. Aurillo, Jr

DEDICATION

To my loving wife Ritz, son Jesse, grandson
Gabe, sisters Elsa and Yuyeen,
sisters-in-law Peachy and Pat, family
and others who taught me all about life

CONTENTS

Acknowledgments   i

1   Why Hypnotism Works!   Page 1

2   The Subconscious Mind   Page 4

3   MindBrain   Page 7

4   A Human Hard Disk   Page 10

5   Self-Hypnotism   Page 13

6   Mind Communication   Page 16

7   The Power In Us   Page 19

8   The Power   Page 23

9   The Samadhi   Page 27

10   Eternity   Page 31

ACKNOWLEDGMENTS

I wish to thank CreateSpace.com
an Amazon company that
enabled printing of this little book
that otherwise would have
had to wait until later

1
WHY HYPNOTISM WORKS!

Hypnotism works whether we believe it does or does not. A person who hasn't traveled in space to the moon may say there's no such thing as a moon. But the heavenly body is there all right independently of what he may say or think. And it is just too bad that there's more people who haven't been to the moon like those few guys who trained to become astronauts in the US Apollo Moon Program in the 1970s.

If we think about it there's quite a lot of people who don't believe in hypnotism or even ask what it is. Some believe in it in one form or another but mostly the type they usually think of is the one performed as stage magic in circuses and variety shows. This is the wrong kind as far as this book is concerned.

If you will observe I use the word hypnotism and not *hypnosis*.

The reason for this is that the term hypnosis is closely associated with medical practice and nowadays we hear of medical procedures performed by doctors using hypnosis as anesthetic. On the other hand the term can relate to entertainment with the term hypnosis as added value in advertisements for a performance. We want to steer clear of these misconceptions to better approach the subject of hypnotism with less fanfare and mental clutter.

Another funny thing about hypnotism is that it is said that it is always done while the subject is asleep. Truth is stranger than fiction. And the truth is that hypnotism or hypnosis, if you will, works while the person is wide awake. It works as the person "hypnotized" eats, sleeps, drives to work and keeps his affairs in order throughout his life. The only time it doesn't work is when the person is dead.

Now, this statement can make anyone think that I'm making it up to sound a little different from other people who talk about it. I'm certainly not making things up nor is this information any different than it is. There is more to our waking hours that's good to know about ourselves as with things that happen to us during our sleeping time. Or, rather, between our waking and sleeping hours.

When a person is awake he is free to do as he chooses, right? Of course. He is able to do this because of his mind. It is his mind that makes his body do things. It's not the other way around. Now, it would certainly be absurd to imagine a person as just a body without a mind. That's not the way we human beings have been brought up to think about ourselves, is it? But when we seriously think about the mind, that's when we begin to have a little problem trying to understand it.

Here, I'm not talking about the issues that characterize human action whether these are good or bad, in other words the problem of good and evil and stuff like that. I'm talking about what actually happens when the mind tells the body to do (or not do) something or anything at all. You may start wondering about the mind being a huge factor in what a person thinks, feels and does. Guess what? You're right. It really is. The mind controls everything. And even the thought precisely of not doing anything in particular, is still the decision of the mind. Creepy.

You'd think that I may have gotten mixed up in my discussion of hypnotism because I've switched to talking about the mind. A person hypnotized while wide awake? Not at all. We're still on the same page, which is about hypnotism.

It's like this. The mind is made up of two parts, the conscious and subconscious parts. I'm almost sure you may have heard of these two terms before. However, it's not really as much about what you've heard as about what these things do to us (think of the person who didn't believe there's a moon for not having stepped foot on it like an astronaut). In fact I'll try to cut down on technical terms to explain things without oversimplifying them. Now then, all of our actions are the end result of the suggestions that have been recorded and stored in our subconscious mind. From the moment a human fetus is crouched motionless in its mother's womb its subconscious mind is recording and storing away all the sensations of sound, touch, warmth, cold, the way it is receiving nutrition, etc.

These sensations are kept there forever. They are like files on a computer that have been saved and may be retrieved at any time; files that you can use to customize your computer programs and activity. The computer can then refer to the files with ease especially if they are set on default mode because those files are clearly understood by its memory.

That explains why a person has, in life, a particular tendency or

2

inclination which is really nothing but the thoughts molded from the information the fetus has acquired and kept in the subconscious mind. If a baby has a hysterical woman for a mother, it will be born with deeply embedded and clearly distinguishable memory of the shrieks and screams of its mom that the baby will associate these with her.

Now, if the human fetus can absorb information it hasn't seen, touched or heard with intentional use of its five senses which it obviously cannot do, then how does it go about getting it? It does it simply by the action of its subconscious mind. If so, then just think how a grown person can absorb gigabytes of information, store it in his subconscious mind and use it when he wants or needs it, whether his intention is good or bad. For the truth is that, any person alive today is actually using his subconscious mind, without even knowing it, for the most part.

When a person eats, drinks, brushes his teeth, goes to bed or gets up in the morning he does it because that is the data or information his subconscious mind is telling him. The person has been so used to getting instructions from this subconscious mind since even before he was born that he doesn't care or bother to think about it. He just prefers to call what he's doing as a "habit."

A habit is of course learned action. And it is the subconscious mind that learns it. If the subconscious mind did not learn it then we would have no idea what it is that we want to do and we would then have to re-learn the whole thing over and over each time we tried to do it even when we had done it many times before with success, because then each act would have been a totally new experience for not having a memory of it in the subconscious mind which is the place to keep it and where to find the information about it. Weird, right?

We take for granted what we consistently do because we are so familiar with it. What we don't know is that each action is triggered by the subconscious mind sending matching information by the trillionth of a second across the nervous system and eventually producing the desired physical activity. This activity can be anything including engaging in conscious thinking and meditating on some ideas, thoughts, images and feelings.

Like a memory card on a computer the subconscious mind keeps data that have been received from embryo to embalmed unless the information on the subject is modified or overwritten, in other words, until the person changes his thoughts about it. Similarly, a computer needs to have programs installed to make the machine do its work. These programs may be updated or deleted and the computer database changes too.

2
THE SUBCONSCIOUS MIND

The subconscious mind works very much like a computer hard drive. What is kept in it is what its user can utilize. But while a computer can store enormous data, work with precision and even be programmed to turn on and off automatically the subconscious mind can do a lot more. As a matter of fact a person is conceived with his subconscious mind automatically turned on, ready to use and it stays that way permanently. It goes off only when the person is dead.

A person born completely blind and deaf would have a very limited idea of the world around him without eyes to see and ears to hear of things in order to know about their appearance, shape, size and color. He could use information through his organs of smell and touch and his subconscious mind will record the information however scant. Such a person will also have obtained data inside his mother's womb as a fetus. However, his experience of the outside world would still be restricted by his physical condition.

A human being born with complete faculties, on the other hand, is infinitely more powerful than a state-of-the-art computer I suppose. Observe that even prehistoric humans could sense danger and take evasive action or fight to the death a perceived aggressor as a natural characteristic of the subconscious mind. If his subconscious mind didn't warn him early enough about the danger, he could be smiling and welcoming the deadly predator with open arms.

What this means for us is that the "programming" of the subconscious mind is complete and does not depend on any "software" if you will. The kind of programming humans have of their subconscious mind is natural to the human condition and doesn't require anything else to start using it.

Education and skills training may enhance the personality of the human being but they don't add more to the subconscious mind.

Let me rephrase that. Education and training do add more to the database of the subconscious mind. But they won't change its nature and capabilities. A coarse and brutal personality may be trained in civilized, formal ways and then transformed into a desirable and much better person. And yet, if the reason for the education is not to overwrite the noxious characteristic then the person may be both arrogant on one hand and kind-hearted on the other, a sort of Jekyll and Hyde personality in one human being. The reason is that he has both characteristics in his subconscious mind.

The subconscious mind is a very useful tool as you can see. It is clear by now that the subconscious mind is a neutral agency of the human being that may be customized to serve our needs. And so when the subconscious mind is filled with happy thoughts even when the current situation is a little bleak, even hopeless, the physiology of the body changes. At quantum level cells in the body are revitalized and become alive even more. Tissues and organs are poised to heal and improve performance.

But when negative thoughts are stored in it like thoughts of murder and mayhem that's when the person is *off-the-wall* if you will, drives himself real nuts and becomes a menace to himself and others. I have a sneaky feeling that this is the reason priests caution their followers to only entertain lofty thoughts and live moral lives to earn salvation. Doctors tell their patients encouraging news about their progress and recovery in a rescue attempt to stave off negative thinking. They understand that a persistent negative attitude can produce more harmful toxic wastes in the body and stymie the treatment. And lawyers as well as police tell citizens to quit stupid thoughts that can get them into trouble with the law.

So, what's with this subconscious mind? We have been talking about it in terms of what it can do. And as I've said above, it's like a computer hard drive but it can do a lot more. And here the similarity stops. We can perhaps begin our study of it by asking another question: is it located in the brain? Or, more precisely, is it found in the right hemisphere of the brain as some researchers believe? I think that to both questions the answer is only partly yes. And this answer only scratches the surface.

You will note that I haven't mentioned the word *brain* up until this point. The reason is that the mind is not synonymous with the brain. Another way of saying it is that the subconscious mind is not the brain. The brain is the physical organ that connects, through the nervous system, to the rest of the physical body with its dizzying and complicated superstructure composed of the circulatory, respiratory, skeletal, muscular, digestive, glandular, metabolic and nervous systems, with their cells, nerve, fiber, ligament etc. Yes, the subconscious mind is found in the brain. But it is also present in the DNA and in every cell of the entire body. It is found in the lowest particles of matter.

It used to be that the protons and neutrons were classified as the lowest units of matter. Well, nowadays they debate about the *higgs bosun* which researchers say is beyond the neutrons and other known lowest particles of matter. This newly-discovered unit is a wavelike form and is almost imperceptible even to the trained scientist and researcher. This wavelike particle is an enigma, a mystery to science that believes that it shouldn't be there. But it is there all right.

What has confounded researchers is the fact that this waveform isn't either physical or non-physical in its elementary properties, but a bit of both. Be that as it may, the consensus is that the waveform is the junction point, the meeting place, the halfway house of the physical and the mental planes, in other words, the material and spiritual worlds. If so, then we may have found the missing link between mind and matter, between body and soul.

Or, between science and religion, one might say. And if this is the case, then we've probably discovered how and why our thoughts can influence our physical body.

3
MINDBRAIN

Researchers say that we use only ten-percent of our brain power in our lifetime and ask what the ninety percent is doing in the meantime? Well, a little clarification is important here because I've observed that the term brain power is used interchangeably with mind power and they happen to be two different things.

As we have seen in our discussion, the mind is not the brain. And again the subconscious mind exists in the DNA and at cellular level in all of the body and not just in the brain. On the other hand, the brain is the organ perched on top of the human body. It doesn't have a ligament or muscle reaching the toe.

Those who study metaphysics believe that the subconscious mind exists not just within the physical body but even *outside* of it. This can be verified scientifically. One way to do it is to place two grandfather clocks side by side together. The pendulum of the clock on the right is swung to the right and the one on the left is swung to the left so that both pendulums are swinging in opposite directions at the same time. Eventually, the pendulums will sway in unison and harmony left to right and back again together as if they didn't initially swing in opposite ways.

Researchers think that this is nature's way of re-establishing harmony or resonance in the universe as a default condition of being. When left untouched and free of human interference the disorder is brought back to unity and perfection, perhaps much like a bodily injury that heals itself eventually. They say this is the law of all things in the universe. I agree.

The conclusion seems to be that mind is a force that operates on a level that doesn't have to deal with the human brain to do it. As such, we may have to quit pointing a forefinger to our head when talking about the mind as if to mean the brain. The brain is an organ of the physical body. On the other hand the mind is non-physical and is part of the mental and spiritual nature of the human being. Note that by "spiritual" I don't necessarily mean religious.

It seems to me then that any other explanation will mean that a person has no subconscious mind. In this scenario the person is just a mass of jumbled flesh, bone and blood and the brain functions organically to direct the physical activity of the body and ensure its survival. But without the subconscious mind the person is really not much different from an animal.

Let me rephrase that one. I said a person cannot be without a subconscious mind. Indeed, everything in nature has a mind. This is the force that gives everything in our environment its existence, shape, size and other attributes. However, while the subconscious mind of the human being will support his body's physiological functioning yet without the education, training and experience to enhance the personality, the human being will remain in the basic survival mode and not much more.

In other words the training is the "updated version" or program of the human hard drive which is the subconscious mind. A brand new computer without the needed programs installed to make it work will not be of much value to us. Similarly, you can imagine a person with a blank subconscious mind or *tabula rasa* aimlessly going about and living without a purpose. That's what happens to the sick and the insane. While their mind isn't totally blank yet there's no stored data or information that are useful to them to make them live complete and useful lives.

The human brain is actually the interpreter of data or information reaching the conscious mind through the five portals which are the senses of seeing, smelling, tasting, hearing and touching. I've mentioned the *conscious mind* to distinguish from the subconscious mind only to explain the activity of the brain. The conscious mind uses the brain as the decoding system to process information preparatory to storing in the subconscious mind.

Scientists and researchers uniformly say that it is in the left hemisphere of the brain that cognitive, deductive and logical processes are happening in every moment that we live while the more abstract, philosophical and artistic attributes of a person are made to manifest through the right hemisphere. I'm inclined to clarify that while logic and reason are the tools of the conscious mind for receiving information the storing of data isn't done in the right hemisphere exclusively. For as we've seen the subconscious mind is present not just in the brain but in every other part of the human body (and even outside of it).

As I've said about the pendulums there is a mysterious quality of the subconscious mind that involves people and things. I think this mysterious bond also explains so-called *butterfly effect* in all of nature.

The butterfly effect is a philosophical cliché used to explain in ordinary terms a concept which says that since all things in nature are one and therefore connected with each other in some way then what occurs at a certain time and place can influence another state or condition of nature in one form or another. A butterfly fluttering its beautiful wings in Japan changing the wind in Argentina? True. That is, if a boiling temper let's say of an intolerant person could affect his heart condition and blood pressure even without his knowing it.

Indeed, a crisis or disaster gripping any country can affect other nations in a variety of ways such as trade and commerce, diplomacy and international relations and in the thinking and attitude of people about the events. And war between and among countries, for example, can involve other nations as happened in World War II. But I'm getting ahead of myself.

It is very likely that the wavelike particle I mentioned earlier that connects everything in nature causes the butterfly effect to occur. In this way the concept of the brain as the seat of power has been redefined. What this means for us is a real understanding of the brain as just the motor that drives the vehicle, which is our physical body, and with the subconscious mind as its fuel.

When you think about it you will sense that the brain is not the number one physical organ the way we thought about it before. The brain is just like a generator to power activity. And like the electric power generator, it needs fuel from the subconscious mind to do it.

4
A HUMAN HARD DISK

Have you ever wondered how a computer hard disk can process every bit of information that has been stored or programmed into it? I mean how fast and precise the information is retrieved when the command is given to display it? It handles it perfectly well as long as the data stored matches the programming software, storage capacity and other requirements for input, memory, retrieval and other stuff that make a computer work well .

But have you given thought about how your subconscious mind works in a similar fashion? Imagine that you've had a pin accidentally prick your leg. You are jolted from the shock of acute stabbing pain burning in the injured area and swear you hadn't felt that kind of sensation before. A deep pinprick always feels like a terrible experience that makes you think you haven't experienced anything like it in your life.

What actually happens is that the nerve cells in the area stabbed have sent a signal in a flash for about a micro-second informing the cortex of the brain about the injury. As the decoder of the stimulus the brain interprets any kind of information sent whether of pain or pleasure. And if it is pain, the type of pain whether abrasive, cutting, stabbing and if the feeling of pain is of short or else lingering duration, as well as its intensity.

At blinding speed unknown to any processor the brain turns out data on what kind of sensation it is. Then the information is sent back to the area of the injury. However, it isn't just sent to the location of the wound but even to your entire body as well. You will observe that the physical pain could involve your emotions too and cause you to have feelings of anxiety and anger about how careless you may have been in not avoiding it. It may also evoke trauma or an abiding fear of pointed and sharp instruments. This is not surprising. Emotional upset can be triggered because the stimulus acts on the subconscious mind which is, as we've said, present in the DNA at quantum level and not just in the brain.

I suppose that the ninety-percent of the brainpower referred to by researchers as the inactive part of the human brain is actually the sum total of the subconscious mind of an individual. Consequently it may be an error to say that this ninety-percent is located in the right brain hemisphere as with the notion that it is inactive. Because it is not. The "ninety-percent" as we've seen is located everywhere at quantum and cellular levels. Those who speak about giving the right brain hemisphere all the credit as well as responsibility for subconscious functioning may tend to underestimate the usefulness and indispensability of the rest of the body.

For instance, how do we characterize the uses of speech, hearing and mobility, if all we can agree on is the superiority of the right brain hemisphere with its ninety-percent power? I think some scholars could be off-the-wall, if you will, when they say that humans have forgotten to use their ninety-percent brain power. Really, it's not their brain that we imagine they're using. It's their mind power. And mind is not brain and vice-versa.

I could be more in keeping with my topic if I say that people do indeed use their subconscious mind with its ninety-percent capacity. The only problem is that they are not aware they are doing it. They don't bother. Or, they may not understand or appreciate its true power, and they don't care. Nevertheless, I'd say that people use their subconscious mind no matter what they do or think. And they'd still be doing it if they even decide to forget all about it.

You can go to bed at night and sleep throughout without thinking of giving instructions to your heart to keep up with the pumping to sustain blood and oxygen supply so your brain stays alive. And you don't have to consciously and deliberately tell your lungs to breathe to keep you from dying in bed, do you?

The autonomic nervous system does it all for you. It gets its default instructions from the subconscious mind. And it's been this way since birth and even before that when you were an embryo. It does seem like some things do their thing even without our knowledge, bidding or even consent, don't they? But then how do you tell if we humans are using our ninety-percent? We may have to engage in metaphysical terms even when we started on layman's terms.

I do believe, however that when we sleep well, eat well and think as well, and when we practice exercises that strengthen the mind and body we do our subconscious mind a big favor. We give it lots of input and data about correct living and thinking. Then it complies with our own requirements as human beings and so responds to our call for help in times of need since it has all the information and resources to help us at such times. An example of this is when we are fleeing from a mugger or killer.

We dash like a marathon runner to try to save ourselves from danger.

How does it happen that we can run like hell away from imminent death, climb a high wall or fence or fight off an attacker with such ferocity and determination as if we had trained ourselves to fight for a life and death situation? Although most people are not professional athletes or martial artists and do not or cannot perform such bodily feats on ordinary days, yet we can do these because elementary knowledge of means to survive are stored and kept in our subconscious mind to be used in actual situations. We do not even have to "type in" or "google search" it. Our subconscious mind automatically tells our body when and how to respond to the crisis or emergency.

It helps to expose our subconscious mind to different scenarios to absorb data that may be helpful to us in life. This is done through education and experience. I believe this is the goal of institutions of learning. The people who raise us as a family have a larger responsibility in helping mold our subconscious mind. Most parents do not realize that the subconscious mind has power. Their action, mannerism and speech are mimicked by their own children who then act and speak like their own parents did before them. And they do so similarly in their own lives in turn.

This "mimicking" will have gone on with *both* parents and children being absolutely clueless the entire time.

5

SELF-HYPNOTISM

I should have titled this chapter as "Hypnotism" instead of "Self-hypnotism". The reason for this is self-evident in my discussion of the subconscious mind.

As the subconscious mind is the repository of the entire knowledge that a person absorbs and which guides him throughout his entire life it may be said that it is what makes him aware of himself as a thinking being. He has self-awareness because of it. However, being certain that one exists is not, I believe, the ultimate goal of a person's life. A person can exist as a living thing like a tree or a cat perhaps but it's quite obvious that this isn't a very noble or inspiring goal for mankind. By its very nature a plant or an animal doesn't even know it exists. But a human being is designed to do more out of his life than eat, sleep and have sex.

A person's subconscious mind is what makes him know about himself, his own nature and environment. Through his seeing, smelling, tasting, hearing and touching, he is able to distinguish what it is that catches his attention. When he pushes his desire to know more he discovers that there is no limit to where he can go both physically and mentally. Human history is filled with stories of how discoverers of continents and new worlds proved this to be true of man as a human organism. And at this very moment modern science is making huge progress in space and time travel with superstring and inter-dimensional technology.

It is this awareness of himself that actually brings knowledge to be processed and stored in the human being's subconscious mind. With more stored knowledge to utilize, the scope of awareness extends even more. Also at this moment full research and development are undertaken by countries on how to tap the subconscious mind for a variety of uses such as in the area of communication, finding lost persons, solving crimes and other purposes. To illustrate, a technique has been actually tested whereby winning lotto numbers are correctly guessed by an individual who tries to read the mind of another person in an experiment in which this second person scans and studies numbers from a deck of cards.

The set of numbers that strongly catches the attention and interest of the second individual will be "read" by the first person who is located a mile away from the second one. This reading will be done by the first individual with eyes closed as he visualizes and captures the lucky numbers with the use of his subconscious mind zeroing in on the numbers mentally selected by the second person. Several tries of this technique have resulted in dramatic guesses. I haven't done it so far but there are claims that a persistent attempt can eventually get the right combinations.

Self-hypnotism is a misnomer. There is no self-hypnotism. All hypnotism are the actual process and experience of receiving all facts, data, knowledge and impressions channeled through the faculties of seeing, smelling, tasting, hearing and touching on their way to be stored and preserved in the eternal repository which is the subconscious mind. You may not realize it but there's a ton of information stored in your subconscious mind and it can include even unwanted impressions such as those relating to sad, unfortunate, negative, hostile or frightful experiences and those involuntarily implanted on your subconscious mind as in the case of brainwashing.

The subconscious mind receives all this information in its crude, raw primitive and original condition. If the person receiving the impression is in a brainwave frequency called *alpha* which is a state of relaxed awareness and daydreaming or in *theta* which is the threshold between waking and sleeping, the information received is firmly rooted in the subconscious mind. So strong is the adhesion of these impressions that it will take a trained hypnotherapist to "brainwash" if you will, the person to have these memories erased from his subconscious mind.

When a person is at these two brainwave frequencies his subconscious mind is easy to train or develop. During these episodes the person acquires the information not through the regular channels of sight, smell, taste, sound and touch. What happens is that these external senses are bypassed and the information goes straight to the subconscious mind. It is said that the external senses are the tools the conscious mind uses as the so-called "gatekeeper" of all incoming information.

If the incoming information doesn't resonate or agree with values and beliefs that have been pre-set and stored in the subconscious mind it will be rejected by the conscious gatekeeper whose job it is to keep unfamiliar impressions out of the subconscious, like an error in a computer display. The idea of the conscious mind as a sort of filtering system is to protect our emotions and preserve the status quo. Any new information that impacts our current belief systems in a way that can upset our sense of well-being and security, and therefore our comfort zone, will be refused entry by the gatekeeper.

However, impressions may successfully enter the subconscious mind unimpeded by the external senses the moment we are deeply relaxed and when we remain suspended between sleep and wakefulness. You may have heard of the report about how an advertisement for popcorn and soda was flashed every after several frames of a movie film that was showing and the moviegoers didn't notice the ad. But a good number of them came out of the movie wanting to get the brand of popcorn and soda that was flashed not really knowing why? The ad was subliminally implanted in their subconscious mind as they relaxed and enjoyed the movie. Their eyes didn't catch it, but their subconscious minds did.

The fact is that the subconscious mind is very receptive to suggestions whenever the physical body and the external senses are relaxed. Psychologists have advised patients to avoid falling asleep in front of the TV because movies with violent themes may be showing as you sit there too relaxed and half-asleep. You may not be aware that your subconscious mind may be subliminally receiving unpleasant and harmful language, images and scenes that may impact your consciousness and make you say or do things that you really don't want to if you had the choice.

While the subconscious mind cannot be told to do something it doesn't want that may derail one's comfort zone it cannot also be stopped from imitating or mimicking anything, and doing it like it was its own original thought or idea, which it is, for having absorbed it. Like a computer hard drive which is undiscriminating, religion and pornography can have their folders peacefully co-exist side by side together on the same library.

I said that the subconscious mind cannot be told to do or not do anything. Of course. When you think of a "stage hypnotist" trying to entertain his audience with an assistant usually a pretty girl being magically told to sleep as she hangs or floats in the air, well, the girl usually does float, with invisible wires or a pole arm to assist in staging the illusion. But don't be fooled that she has been placed under the "spell" of the artist. Nobody can be subjected under the power of anyone unless he or she agrees to it. The person supposedly hypnotized, in this case the girl, goes about obeying the artist's instructions. In reality, she doesn't do any of that. Instead, what she does comes entirely from her subconscious mind that she has freely given temporary expression. She is obeying her own mind, not the magician's.

6
MIND COMMUNICATION

Mind or mental communication is the exchange of messages between two or more people using the power of their own will to influence each other's thoughts. It is a wordless exchange of messages usually between or among a group of people who believe in mind power and have kindred thoughts about it. But mind communication is not just about people mentally trying to communicate with each other's thoughts.

Properly speaking, it is about the process of utilizing the subconscious mind as an energy field in order to bring forth into physical reality a thought form initialized by the conscious mind as a planned created thing.

Mind communication can be accomplished if someone has a desire so great and a talent so strong at visualizing images with such clarity and power you'd think the image has come to life before your own eyes. Mind communication, however, is discussed here only to the extent as it affects or influences suggestions made upon the subconscious mind.

When we do think that our subconscious mind carries information on everything about us then we must agree that the subconscious mind of others would have the same capability, characteristics and properties as that of ours too. After all, it is the same mind, the same energy field from which we draw our own vitality and subconscious power.

From this statement comes the realization that mind communication is as natural as imagination is. The subconscious mind is really a vast source of mental energy that is available to us all. Students of the mind sciences are trained to relax and use imagination to create mental pictures of desired outcomes in the physical world. Napoleon Hill has said that if you consistently have a mindset about getting rich as a lifetime goal and this thought is a fixed part of your personality never to be taken lightly, and if this persistent thought is fueled with an unflinching and unwavering commitment to the goal of eternal abundance, then you will inescapably become rich. Your mind has no way to go except in the direction of getting rich.

Conversely, if you think of becoming a hobo or beggar then your subconscious mind will oblige and give you what you desire which is to live a life of sloth and stupidity. It will tell you that you don't want to get paid for decent work and earning a livelihood isn't necessary or even good. And so, you will begin to feel like you're through with your own life. Life will suddenly become useless and incomprehensible to you and ultimately you will give it up in order to wander around as a filthy tramp, in conformity with your subconscious desire. Your subconscious mind will obey your wishes because your desires are real images stored in your mind ready for you to use when you want them.

The subconscious mind is a neutral force that you can use in your life in whatever way and for any purpose.

Consequently, mind communication is about tapping the vast resource of archetypes and symbolisms in the subconscious mind to create something and bring it into realization in the physical world. And it may be used for good or ill because the subconscious mind doesn't judge what it is doing and isn't concerned with the morality or uprightness of your decisions. It just gives you the information that you need and then, depending on your desire, it will energize your will and turn the archetype into something real in the outer world. If the information is not in its database it will give you an error page just like your laptop does. Cool, right?

Mind communication can be verified by tests as in the long distance reading of winning lotto numbers that I've mentioned. However, a more dramatic method of verification is in the area of sympathetic magic. In this method the voodoo practitioner, guru or shaman, can place a curse upon a person by performing a ritual while touching or stroking a piece of cloth, jewelry or any personal accessory of the victim that is constantly used or carried by that person on his/her body. The "curse" or evocation of evil will attach itself upon the personal accessory and produce illness, bad luck or even death upon the victim.

The term sympathetic magic is used to denote a connection between the shaman and his victim that is established through the personal accessory as link or intermediary.

Mind communication always utilizes the subconscious mind as an energy field in order to produce the desired results in the physical world, whether that goal is to silently reach the mind of another person in order to send a message to them, or to influence the vibration of the energy field in order to turn a concept or idea into physical form. As you can probably imagine, there is an enormous amount of activity in the mental world as there is in the physical world. And going by our definition of terms it is clear that there isn't anything you can see in the physical world that didn't originally begin as an idea or thought in the mental (or subconscious) world.

I suspect that the subconscious mind indeed is a real dimension of existence in and of itself and it molds the human nature of individuals whether they are awaiting birth (or rebirth) as infants, or, for having lived on earth for most of their lives, have passed on in death.

We may have to ask ourselves: If there is such a vast mental database in the whole of creation and this huge invisible resource is interspersed with the physical world as seems to be the case, then how is it that we don't feel anything if we are really surrounded by all these archetypes, forms and ideas?

The answer is, we do.

We think these archetypes don't impinge on our consciousness but they always do. The truth, however, is that we don't give much attention to it simply because in the majority of cases we don't believe in it. We take for granted that the invisible world isn't real for being just that--invisible. Some folks who are off-the-wall could arguably say that oxygen isn't probably real because they can't see it. That's fine with them and others like them. Yet, we could die in minutes if we were to be deprived of oxygen in the air we breathe. Or, they could say they don't believe the wind is real until they see the swaying of the leaves in the trees caused by the breeze.

How then, can we use the brain in order to communicate with the subconscious mind?

We have so far discussed that the brain is not the mind, let alone the subconscious mind. We have gone as far as saying that this subconscious mind is an energy field, an entity unto itself implying thereby that it has a certain autonomy and operates independently of our control. The implication of this statement is that we do not own it like we own our house or our insurance policy. We cannot appropriate it as our own property even when we can use it in a personal way. This is a real paradox.

To be able to use the subconscious mind for this purpose we have to get our brain to initialize our contact with it. Now, didn't we say that it always impinges on our consciousness and establishes contact with us on a regular basis? Yes, indeed, we are always in contact with our subconscious mind. But more precisely, it is always in contact with us. But unless we observe certain steps to harness its power we may not be able to know what it does and how it works.

To get the power of the subconscious mind to work to our benefit we must first admit that it is real. I suppose there'd be no use getting our hands on something that isn't there to take in the first place. I mentioned that although we can feel its presence and influence we nonetheless always choose not to mind it for one reason or the other. So, it seems that to start us getting into business with the subconscious mind we have to open our senses, feelings and intuition so we may experience what it is telling us.

7
THE POWER IN US

In the last chapter I said that to begin using the power of the subconscious mind we have to open our senses which are our important attributes as human beings. In philosophy there is a cliché that says when you close a door you open another one. So then, as applied to our topic you may want to figure what to do with our five external senses. Do we open or close them? We do both.

Here's the deal. The five senses are the portals used by the conscious mind to receive impressions and pass them on for storing in the subconscious mind. We have to close them to stop their activity in receiving impressions every microsecond of our lives. The idea is to give the mind a rest and time to refocus. Let me rephrase that. The mind really needs no rest. It's the body that does. But refocusing is something else.

By closing our five senses while remaining conscious (to distinguish from closing our eyes while we are asleep) we begin getting to know the subconscious mind. The fun starts here...

This is the mind that knows everything about you since being born. And if you stay silent with eyes closed even further, this mind will tell you where your life is headed from hereon. This is also the stuff that knows everything about other people, places and events. There is no time, no day or night here. You are in the presence of the consciousness that connects with the mind of all things that have been, are, and will be. You are in the presence of eternity. You can call it deity, life force, Almighty or whatever you like. How you call it will not change anything about it. What is it? I have no words to say it. There is none. It just is.

But before you start closing your eyes while you're walking down a busy street and exposing yourself to danger from rapists and killers you must know that to successfully contact the subconscious mind you must do it while you are free of the hassles of your daily life.

It is very important for you to learn that when you start contacting the subconscious mind you will have to commit yourself to doing it on a regular basis. It is in the consistency of the practice that you will know if you've met with some success from your experience. It's like when you embark on a program of physical exercise you must give it time to see the results. Dr Robert Anthony says that we do have enough common sense to know that if you plant a tree you can't stomp and thrash the ground demanding to see if the seed has sprouted after burying it in soil. You must give it time to nurture and grow.

Closing the eyes and breathing slowly bring calm and peace to your whole being. You can stop reading now and try closing your eyes. Observe carefully that it is a little dark beneath your eyelids especially if the light in the room is dim. But keep your eyes closed, steady and relaxed and you will perceive a string of thoughts in all their texture, color and clarity as they parade in front of your mind. It is a cavalcade of images that reflect the predominating thoughts you may have of the day from the most insignificant and mundane to the most pressing and urgent. The purpose of this little exercise is to show you that your mind is real and how you may have been taking this for granted.

The ancient philosophers call this state of mind *pratyahara*. Whether your thoughts dance in merriment or growl in grief as they parade themselves before your closed eyes, you are asked not to interrupt them or in any way hinder, obstruct or put a stop to their activity. You are deemed successful in this mind exercise when you can allow these thoughts to pass through the screen of your mind unmolested. Sounds easy? Try it.

Your mind doesn't keep still. It is always processing information consisting of images, sounds or other types of stimuli. When you try to subdue it that's when it resists and crowds out your thoughts with even more thoughts. Your mind is always active even when you are asleep and totally relaxed. Think of a stray dog sniffing around the garbage dump. Your mind is like that except that the dog stretches itself to rest after a while. Your mind doesn't.

Pratyahara prepares the subconscious mind for the next type of mind exercise. In this second stage you are to imagine a specific object and then focus on it to the exclusion of all other things. Think of a lighted candle for example. Visualize it in front of you in a dark room. It burns steadily with clearly defined features, a tall, white and thick candle with an orange-yellow flame. As soon as you have it in your mind stay with the image for as long as you can while remaining as relaxed as possible. The cell phone and other gadgets should be turned off. Later, you can make the mental picture even more alive by imagining you are so close to it and can feel the warmth of the candle flame. Or, you can visualize yourself sticking a finger into the fire and jerking your hand from the heat. When you can keep this vision of the chosen object and prevent other thoughts from intruding you have succeeded in this exercise which is called *dharana*. When doing this you will observe that other thoughts keep pressing in for your attention like where to get the money to pay the bills, what to do with a nagging parent or boss or a very bad neighbor. Just smile and let go of these thoughts peacefully as in pratyahara. Do not try to put them off forcefully. If you do you won't succeed I guarantee. Wait until they're gone and start over. You will know that you are succeeding because you will sense very definitely that your other thoughts are gone and there is a distinctive feeling to it.

The third step is when you can let your mind go absolutely blank. There is no parade of unbridled thoughts. And there is no focusing on a single image. There is just nothing in there. This is very hard to do. I said that your thoughts can press hard for attention as you do the second exercise. It's because you can rely on the chosen image as your shield, your armor in warding off the troublesome thoughts during the second exercise. The "shield" seems to effectively draw attention away from the troublemakers. But when there is no shield as in the third exercise it's like fighting naked in a brawl or a free-for-all.

However, you must begin to learn the third step anyway and keep at it until you master it. This third exercise is called *dhyana*. This should not be attempted, however, unless you have developed your skills with the first two steps. You are not required to be an expert in those first two exercises. But neither are you expected to go even a tiny bit of success with the third without substantial effort, along with the failures, plus a measurable success in the first two stages. In my experience I've found out that the most difficult for me to do is the second one as I've described above. However, it is probably just a matter of attitude because I think difficulty arises when the exercises are interrupted and most especially if they are not quickly resumed after a pause for any length of time.

8
THE POWER

The power that I've been discussing here is the power of the subconscious mind which as we have said is a vast energy field that encompasses all of creation. By "creation" I'm not talking of it with a capital "C" to skip any religious meaning or implication. I'm just referring to it in the ordinary sense which means the making of things, whether it involves making them out of nothing or out of something else even if the latter just happens to be another created thing. And again, whether these elements or ingredients of creation are perceivable by the senses or not.

It has been said that the power of the subconscious mind is the same force that organizes the universe and holds the galaxies and planets together to keep them from colliding with one another. It is the same power that gives the earth gravity so we won't just float skyward when we go out the door of our house to report for work or go to school every morning. It is the same invisible thing that commands our heart to automatically pump blood and oxygen, or the digestive system to convert food into energy, the respiratory system to make us breathe even when we're not aware of it such as when we're asleep. It keeps and maintains balance in all of nature so that we heal and recover our good health whenever we're sick. And it maintains resonance whenever there is discord and imbalance. Remember the pendulums?

In as relatively a short time as fifty years ago the struggle for better recognition between the creationists and the evolutionists was so intense they'd swear they had all the answers to man's most important questions. Both of these schools of thought have had a huge following (they still do) because their arguments were accepted well by their followers. They still are. When you think about these two institutions you cannot help but dwell on the subject about beginnings or simply, about creation. What came from which? Which came from what? When? And stuff like that.

Also, advocates of the *big bang* principle of creation have made their own scene with their system about the beginning of things even as the creationists and evolutionists are up in arms defending their individual turf from imagined encroachment of their respective enclaves. The big bang system of thinking frowns upon the two institutions and says that instead of anything else the whole thing started as a result of a great cosmic cataclysm eons ago. Gosh! Why do they always speak of a beginning? Haven't anyone listened to Liv Ullman's song "The World Is A Circle"?

You can take a long look at a circle and you'll observe there is really nothing to indicate the beginning and consequently the point of ending in the figure, right?

"The world is a circle without a beginning
And nobody knows where it really ends

"Everything depends on where you, are
In the circle that never begins,
Nobody knows where the circle ends".

The end of course is the opposite of a beginning just like left is the opposite of right, black is the opposite of white, day the opposite of night, and so on. One cannot be without the other. The presence of opposites is essential to the manifestation of things. And conflict is eternally present in the life of a human being. Think of a film, a western movie for example, that you can watch from beginning to end where everything seems all right when the film starts with a stagecoach loading passengers and luggage and then off it begins its journey as the title of the film and the names of the stars are flashed on the screen. Then, for the next two hours the film shows the horses and stagecoach sweeping through hillsides and desert sands with the film showing nothing else but scenes of the stagecoach and its agonizing passengers and the vast territory as background.

There is no highway robbery, no interception of the traveling party, no gunfights, no outlaws, bandits, Mexicans, no Indians, nothing. Then the coach arrives uneventfully at the destination which is a distant town crowded with cowboys, a sheriff and a saloon. That's when the movie says "The End". For two hours you've been watching the stagecoach as it maneuvered over rough and scorching terrain evading rattlesnakes and enduring the searing heat of the desert, and there is no brigandage, banditry or even the obscene language of the bad guys ruining the day of the hero and the pretty lady? Where are the *gringos* anyway? Nothing wrong with these guys. What's so wrong is the movie itself for not having the conflict, the adversaries or opposing characters in it. Like real life itself a story must have its elements of struggle, misfortune, conflict and pain.

The point of this example is the possibility that there may not really be a beginning and consequently an ending to all things. And instead of adhering blindly to inexplicable notions of a beginning and sometimes an even more outrageous end, why not agree on what we have at the moment, which is that things and especially living things, have been and will remain around a little while longer than your conscious mind can possibly imagine.

It is when we subscribe to ideas that have been traditionally fixed in our mind by the creationists, evolutionists and "big-bangers" about how things got started that we then try explaining these things to ourselves. And then we find to our dismay that these concepts are impossible and even absurd. We think that those pioneering thoughts are great. And they are. But for being unable to paint a clear picture so that we may be able to form a coherent structure for the sake of our own belief systems, we are stuck and we get confused. We are shaken because things have suddenly altered our comfort zone and we are forced to pretend to accept what doesn't fit into our belief system.

But changes do happen to us and our environment. Cells in the bodies break down and are replaced by new ones. We put on fresh clothes daily, eat newly-prepared food and start another day every day. However, these are changes, and not beginnings.

If you believe that when a human being dies and his body rots in the grave but his mind does not and instead awaits rebirth in another body then you can say that there has been a transformation in that person's life. In other words, he isn't undergoing a beginning, only a change. That person may have been around for a while and now he could be "shopping" around for a body. But what if this rebirthing thing is neither true nor even practical what happens then? Well, what happens is that it is still a change for him and not a beginning. That change involves a transformation from a being with a physical body as a man or a woman to an entity enmeshed in the great subconscious mind in all of existence and of all time.

So what may become our challenge right now apparently is not as much about being certain that the egg came first before the chicken, as it is in agreeing that there is in this world a thing called egg on one hand, and another object called chicken, on the other. And from this we should be cranking our recipes to cook a really smart menu out of these raw materials. When you look at it from this perspective you'll be surprised that perhaps you may have been wasting your time in the kitchen fumbling with those things instead of doing what should have been done with them right away.

Doing the three mind exercises I briefly described earlier on a regular basis and making it a consistent part of life works wonders for anyone so inclined. Why do it? The immediate benefit is to silence one's mind. What do you experience when the mind is so "silenced"? We do not actually observe it and disregard it if we do, but our mind's ceaseless activity causes thoughts and impressions to influence us every second of our lives. We do not think this is unusual or even real because it has been happening since we can remember and believe this is only natural and nothing can change it. Mainstream religion is against the practice of exploring the mysteries of the inner mind preferring to shepherd its flock with man-made stricture and dogma.

But a person should be interested in controlling his own thoughts, and one who isn't so inclined to this is therefore easily "controlled" by others even when the controlling is possible only because he has agreed to the suggestions made by others. The thoughts that randomly "proliferate" in our minds are the default sounds and images that we have stored in our subconscious mind willingly or even involuntarily when we are in a relaxed state and our brainwave frequencies are in *alpha* and *theta*. We can change these thoughts by overriding them with a mindset that promotes good health and well-being. When the mind is brought to stillness the healing of the body's cells, tissues and organs is accelerated thus giving the sick person better and quicker chances of recovery. Also, the practitioner acquires the ability to remain calm and detached yet alert and involved in any crisis situation.

9

THE SAMADHI

Anyone reading this book may think that I'm discussing a subject that's far removed from the topic of hypnotism. The truth is that hypnotism is a topic that's in the heart of the subconscious mind just as much as your toenail and your scalp are parts of the same physical body you have although located on it's opposite ends. If you pull either or both of them you'll feel pain so intense you don't know what's happening or where its coming from. You don't care if it is coming from the love-handles or middle ear. All you know is that your body is in pain and your concern is only about getting relief from the discomfort.

Obviously, I'm talking about the way the subconscious mind connects with all things and parts of things in all of existence. When you do the three mind exercises I have outlined you will, after a time, be ready for the *samadhi* or the union of your subconscious mind with the greater mind in eternity. You can call the greater mind any name you want like god, being, ultimate reality, cat, whatever. We are interested in your experience with the union. This goal of uniting with eternity is the same thing in point of experience whether you're a white man, a yellow man, red man, a black man, brown man etc.

The protocol in attaining union I'm afraid may vary as the cliché about having many paths to a single destination goes, as it were. In any event it is emphasized that the physical body and its external senses must be relaxed so that the journey of the mind may go unimpeded. The aim is to stop the senses and the way to do this is to descend into the lower *alpha* and *theta* brainwave frequencies where the gatekeeper's turf ends and eternity begins. These frequencies are beneath the level or stage of wakefulness called *beta*. When you have attained some measure of proficiency in the descent you will be able to do it at will. Begin by focusing all your attention upon the top of your head placing all your awareness in that area. After a while you may feel some warmth on your scalp and a tingling sensation there. Relax your scalp. Do this for some minutes then move your attention next to your forehead and concentrate upon it as if your forehead were the only single part of your body there is. As before, relax and spend a few minutes while you feel the warmth and tingling sensation on the forehead indicating that your mind is stimulating that area of your body. Then move your awareness to your eyes. Imagine drawing two circles around your eyes large enough to enclose your eyeballs. Put all your consciousness there and relax both eyes.

Repeat this sequence of fixing the attention and relaxing for a period of one to three minutes upon each part then moving from that part of your body to the next. Do it with your cheeks, mouth and ears. Then do this with your neck shoulders, upper arms, lower arms and hands. Next, move on to your chest and back and feel the clothes touching your skin. Move down to your abdomen and then to your thighs, knees, calves, legs and feet. Do not hold your breath at any moment when you're doing this although breathing must be slow and even-paced. You will notice that as you go on with the exercise random thoughts will fight for space to get your attention. You knowledge of *dharana* will greatly help in warding off these unwanted thoughts as you focus on each particular area of your body at the moment.

This focusing and relaxing exercise will acquaint you with your subconscious mind. If practiced regularly, it will show you the neutral and impersonal nature of the subconscious mind. What this means for you is that your subconscious mind will obey your wishes whether they are positive or negative. It will not urge or command you to do things good or bad because, on the contrary, it is you that commands it to do these things, not the other way around. Some people can attribute omnipotent qualities or higher powers of the subconscious mind, and they are right about it. But it doesn't mean that because of such powers you must kneel before it and supplicate with your subconscious mind so it will be pleased to give you what you want. Here's the secret to getting what you want:

You must see in your mind's eye what it is that you want. You must imagine the thing complete with all details about the object like size, shape, color, and smell. Furthermore, you should imagine and feel that you already have it in your life, now and at this very moment. There are reasons for this. One, the subconscious mind does not judge you whether you have more that you should want more of whatever it is you want. Or have less that you should deserve to have it more than others. Two, it cannot tell if in fact you already have it now, or not at the moment. This is probably why some rich people become richer and some of the poor become poorer still not so much on the point of inequality and injustice as with a lack of true understanding of the power of the subconscious mind.

As we've said the subconscious mind is the source of creation and it gives to the physical world that which was incubated in the mental world. We also said that the subconscious mind is neutral, objective and is so undiscriminating that it doesn't care or even want to know if the thing desired is already manifested in physical reality. But we are getting ahead of ourselves.

Getting our wishes manifested in the material world is a by-product of the three mind exercises done with focus and relaxation. But whether the materialization of our desires is only a side issue or an ultimate goal in itself it must be done only with the observance of the protocol. The mind exercises must always be performed together with the exercises on focusing and relaxation. You will ultimately realize that all these exercises are just one whole system to train ourselves to attune to our subconscious minds. When you have attained proficiency in it you will get the feeling that you've become the real you, not the kind of you that you knew before. It's not the same thing as saying you have become a different person either which you can never be.

You will think clearly, and you'll find that you love to do things and this gives you satisfaction that wasn't there before. Your food will taste differently. Your speech becomes well-mannered and directed and you are certain about things that you weren't as positive before. You are now working with the greatest computer system in the entire world and beyond. You can never be influenced by anyone and anything. You cannot be hypnotized except as you accept and agree to it.

At first you will struggle with the mind exercises especially if you haven't had any similar training before. This is to be expected and it is suggested that looking forward to experiencing the struggle should be avoided because this will program the subconscious mind to accept the difficulty and will oblige the student-practitioner with that "command" or suggestion and give him precisely that. The practitioner should dwell instead on the descent to the lower frequencies, the relaxation of the physical body and the control of his thoughts especially in applying *dharana* correctly and effectively.

In the majority of cases there is no marked change in the practitioner's feeling and observation. He/she will say they have experienced something although unsure of what it was. We know this is not true and the practitioner could be making up something in order to impress especially if the exercises are done in a group or class. Months or even years of doing it can pass and still nothing can actually happen. But when it does the practitioner intuitively knows that his subconscious mind was, in that time, preparing him for the experience of *samadhi* or union with the greater mind. The initial feeling is physical, not mental or spiritual. The practitioner gets the sensation of being held in the grip of something although the hold is not so tight, hostile or even uncomfortable. The pressure is just right for almost anyone to feel. Also, there is a sensation of coldness of the whole body although it's not something that will make you want to put on sweaters or cover yourself with a blanket like on a cold night.

The practitioner must be warned that when this happens he/she should not panic. It's because panic produces fear. Or aggravates it. And fear is a negative emotion. Being afraid is bad enough but panicking is worse because the fear is compounded by the rioting inside the mind of the victim. In the history of mankind I don't think that anything good came out of panicking. I mean, nobody got wealthier or healthier by living in constant panic of something. My mother probably holds the world record of panicking over just about anything and lives out her life in sickness and pain caused by her sad and negative approach to life.

At this point when the practitioner is overcome with fear he must know how to dissipate it by overriding it with agreeable thoughts unless he/she is skilled in *dhyana* and succeeds in banishing the feeling of fear without having to overwrite it with other thoughts or images just by keeping the mind blank until the fear is gone.

10
ETERNITY

The fear that usually haunts the practitioner at this point in the exercises is really the fear of the unknown. It is the common experience of people to be afraid of that which isn't defined in human terms because we feel that an "unknown" enemy usually ghosts and disembodied entities are always lurking somewhere ready to harm us without any means to defend ourselves not knowing the adversary for what he or it can and cannot do to us. In these exercises we are asked not to associate the unknown with some kind of enemy, let alone an evil one. Doing this always causes fear which is negative as we've pointed out before.

But few people quite actually understand it.

If you have been attentive enough you will realize that the subconscious mind is a flexible thing and so will "obey" your wishes. That said, there is no need to be afraid to dive into it in order to explore and get to know it. It is your own thoughts of evil that you carry in the back of your mind that you should be afraid of. If you approach the subconscious mind especially at the stage of its union with the greater mind with these thoughts bugging you then you will have a reason to prepare to be afraid because your own negative thoughts will be amplified by the subconscious mind which, for being a creative force, will produce more of it thus driving you real nuts in fear for your own safety and sanity.

The solution to this is to stop being afraid. This is easier said than done I admit. But if you succeed and get the hang of it, the rest is easy. Some years back I went to a healer in Tacloban City in the Philippines to have a tooth pulled by natural and non-medical means. This meant that the healer was not a dentist and there were no dental equipment and laboratory to do this. I went in because my dentist was not available and didn't like to pull

31

teeth that were abscessed and painful in any case. But I had another reason to do it. I wanted to find out for myself if the natural tooth extraction was real or even possible. The healer, a young man, looked straight and clean almost like a college student trying to earn a degree (which he was I later learned). He didn't droop and talk like a shaman or voodoo practitioner and didn't murmur prayers or secret incantation to the wind, spirits or other. He gently breathed on the top of my head and this gesture made me relax. I could sense he was breathing on my head three times and the breath got a little cooler each time. This surprised me a little bit knowing that a breath is usually warm when the person breathing is so close by as the healer was to me. Now, this anomaly of the breath caused me to worry a little for not being able to find an explanation for it.

The worry soon metamorphosed into fear of what was happening. Now, I didn't have to be afraid as I don't really believe I would have died right there on account of a breath of ice, now did I? Yet, there I was being afraid of the unknown. Then it happened. I started to have the unmistakable experience of an intolerable toothache that made my mucous membranes flood tears and a nose-drip. I felt like my head would crack open. A toothache is so violent you'd give anything to avoid it. Quickly, I thought of a plan to save myself from further trouble. I reckoned that if it was the emotion of fear, my being terrified of the unknown, that started the pain to manifest then I had hoped that banishing that fear could just as true eliminate the pain that it had caused.

Before I could think of another reason to fear something else, which was about any chance that my plan could fail I proceeded to implement it right away. How? I started a silent monologue in my mind saying that "since this was entirely my decision to seek a healer instead of going to a regular dentist and using appropriate dental care and treatment then I have no one else to lay blame on but myself." I continued mentally saying: "and if the penalty for this lapse of judgment is suffering and even death then I accept it." I added a very brief epilogue which said: "And in accepting the consequences, I wish to declare that I'm not doing it because I have a perverted attitude about pain and suffering but only a realistic sense of responsibility on my part."

Then, I let it go. Miraculously, the horrible toothache vanished leaving me smiling but still with tears and the nose-drip. Here's what I learned: The sensation of pain of whatever nature and type is *emotional*, not physical. My evidence is this experience that I've narrated and which I won't ever forget. The real proof is the fact that when the pain abruptly disappeared following my monologue there was no trace or hint of sensitivity to pain around the gums and tissue or any other part of my mouth which there might have been no matter how faint. The offending tooth was extracted with the healer holding it out on his palm for me to see just after breathing on my scalp a third time but before I began wondering about the cold breath and before I started fearing the unknown and then feeling the pain.

I suppose the toothache vanished when I figuratively stood up to confront the fear that was the source of the pain. For some reason I instinctively knew that it was the emotion of fear that was giving life and fueling the painful experience. This negative emotion was denied expression when I decided to stop being afraid of the unknown thus halting the pain as its physical manifestation. This story is told here only to show that when the subconscious mind is approached with a particular vibratory frequency it will come back with the same frequency so that a vibration of peace and happiness for example will make the subconscious mind respond with the same frequency that fosters peace and happiness. By rising up from negativity and thus leaving the vibratory frequency where the emotion of fear resides I turned the tables on the negative emotion of fear as well as its by-product in the form of a physical symptom which was the toothache.

Masters of the mind exercises as well as that of focus and relaxation have said that during *samadhi* their consciousness is able to leave their physical body to travel anywhere in space and time. They have not failed to mention that when traveling in one's consciousness thus leaving the body behind the mind traveler should always keep a pleasant and positive disposition. The reason is that in the higher mental realms the process of manifesting anything is instantaneous. They warn that if the practitioner has not taken to serious studying and practicing of the mind exercises he/she may meet with failure and even danger. A person with an undisciplined or overactive imagination can automatically create forms in the mental world that could terrify him and weaken his will without his even knowing it thus defeating any purpose in undertaking the traveling of the consciousness.

When you experience the sensation of being moderately "gripped" or embraced, if you will, along with the feeling of coldness enveloping the entire body you know you are in the midst of the eternal mind. You also know that your mind has prepared you for this occasion and so you should only dwell on pleasant and lofty thoughts. I do not mean by this that you should think of heaven, holy people or saints or churches. Think only of good thoughts. If I may be explicit enough about it, I'd say *feel* only good feelings. And among the feelings worthy of being practiced I would say gratitude stands highest in the order of ideal thoughts. When feeling grateful we are mysteriously brought closer to having permanent feelings of happiness, contentment and peace even when the environment seems to be chaotic and our lives are becoming disordered independently of whoever might have caused it.

When you sense that you have become less and less concerned with the noise and even mild sounds around you as you are engaged in *dharana* or *dhyana* the "grip loosens" but you remain where you are and you experience a stillness that you can describe as amusing. It's like saying you never even had any reason to be afraid of the unknown in the first place. This is the "unknown" that you won't mind knowing. You will, as you progress in training, realize that it seems it is really the subconscious mind that is grateful to you that you have contacted it so that your life may be fulfilling with its resources it is giving you for the taking. You will discover that those "virtues" about goodness, uprightness or loftiness being offered by moralists and religionists are "sins" hiding behind sheep's clothing of conventionality and economy.

You will happily know that from now on there is something that protects, cushions the impact and comes to your aid anytime you need it. It has all the answers that you want, the resources that you must use to create or finish a job or mission that requires your attention. It will do its job no doubt about it. It is you that must initiate and maintain contact for you to be able to savor the abundance of its resources instead of flipping, flopping, fumbling or platitudinizing about gods, heroes, beginnings, endings, and whatever the news tell you about your community, society, the laws and your neighbor's bad humor.

ABOUT THE AUTHOR

Frank Q. Aurillo, Jr is a middle-aged gentleman who lives and works in the Philippines. He has a wife, son and grandson and a cat named Junior. He loves music and played with a band in college during the 1960s as lead guitarist and vocalist. He is a lawyer and spends most of his hours researching on philosophical and political issues.

www.ingramcontent.com/pod-product-compliance
Lightning Source LLC
Chambersburg PA
CBHW030548290526
45786CB00004B/1916